JACK KEROUAC AND THE DECLINE OF THE WEST

Jack Kerouac and the Decline of the West

An Essay by

Semmelweis

ROGUE SCHOLAR

@RogueScholarPr

ISBN: 979-8-6674-3753-6

Cover photograph:
Jack Kerouac Naval Reserve Enlistment, 1943
Public domain, courtesy of Wikimedia Commons

Contents

INTRODUCTION

I saw the best minds of my generation destroyed by Allen Ginsberg

Jack Kerouac is not a writer one would expect to find being discussed in right-wing circles, except perhaps as an example of what Julius Evola called "*America Negrizzata.*" One of the more famous passages from Kerouac's best known work, *On The Road*, is this one:

> "At lilac evening I walked with every muscle aching among the lights of 27th and Welton in the Denver colored section, wishing I were a Negro, feeling that the best the white world had offered was not enough ecstasy for me, not enough life, joy, kicks, darkness, music, not enough night... I wished I were a Denver Mexican, or even a poor overworked Jap, anything but what I was so drearily, a 'white man' disillusioned."

That was published in 1957, written in 1951. Kerouac thus seemed to exemplify the phenomenon of what Norman Mailer called "the White Negro" in an essay of that title published just a few months before *On The Road*. At the time, this tendency stemmed in part from whites listening to jazz music. In later decades, it would grow even stronger, first in rock n' roll and R&B, and then in the subculture of hip-hop music, which is now no longer a subculture at all but entirely mainstream and global.

When I was in high school in the 1990s, looking for answers to the hows and whys of life as adolescents do, I found the writings of the Beat Generation. My friends and I had already absorbed the neo-hippy ethos of the grunge scene, and so we were were already primed to receive the antecedent anti-wisdom of *The Sixties*. Sex-drugs-and-rock n' roll was the prefab rebellion, already tested on previous generations of socially engineered American youth. We were corralled right into it by our pop culture icons, just as they themselves had been when they were young, like some sort of multi-generational child abuse cycle. We were lost, because we were GenX latchkey kids who were raising ourselves on television and microwave food, and everything we thought we knew about life, culture, art, politics, and rebellion came to us from the Boomers who programmed the media we consumed.

GenX in the 90s had bands but no writers. 80s teenagers had Bret Easton Ellis and Jay McInerney, but we had nobody except maybe Henry Rollins, and even he had a band first. So we had to look back to an earlier time, when people could still write, because they had still been able to get a decent education.

Of the Beat writers, the only one who could actually write was Jack Kerouac. William Burroughs was always more interesting as a thinker and as a character himself than as a writer. Most of his "novels" are not worth reading and are frequently disgusting. Allen Ginsberg had some talent, but he was always more of a celebrity and an activist, which is a polite way of saying "attention whore." Both Burroughs and Ginsberg were the type who like to talk about being writers and poets more than they like actually doing the work. As for the rest, the lesser lights of the Beat movement, some of them were real writers and artists, and some were just hangers on, but none produced any stellar work that holds up as well as Kerouac's best writing, of which there is a lot.

I read all those guys in my teens and twenties, and a lot of other people like them. A few endure as having value beyond being part of a rebellious and resentful adolescent pose — Camus, for his conscience; Bukowski, for his honesty — but most do not. And it's interesting that those who do endure often have some connection to the Classical tradition in one way or another. Bukowski couldn't stand modern music and listened only to classical, while Camus wrote his doctoral thesis on Christian theology and Neoplatonism.

When it came to writing, Kerouac *did the work*, as Steven Pressfield would say. He boasted of already having written a million words when he was in his early twenties, and his archives bear this out. That was before his first published novel, 1950's *The Town and the City*, which is largely forgotten or ignored today because it wasn't written in the mad-dash "spontaneous prose" style of most of his later works. Too bad for the ignorant, because it's one of Kerouac's best books.

Jack Kerouac is important because he occupies a crucial, pivotal point in American culture, and American decline. I could justifiably say Western decline instead, because Kerouac's influence is global, and because American decline is largely a subset of Western decline. But Kerouac is a quintessentially *American* writer, in a way that very few writers who are merely located in America are, and he belongs in that rarefied group of American writers who tell us something about ourselves as a nation. Before Kerouac there were Fitzgerald,

Emerson, and Twain. After? *Après moi, le déluge*, as his very last piece of writing was titled.

In looking at Kerouac's life and art today, it's important to understand that post- World War 2 America was divided between two contradictory moods. On the one hand, there was a feeling of celebration and optimism because we had won the war and were now the most powerful nation on earth. But there was also a deep sense of malaise and doom because of the horrors of the war, culminating in the detonation of the first atomic bombs, which then entered the public consciousness as the likely instruments of armageddon. Among intellectuals, this latter mood predominated, not least of all because intellectuals tend to be depressives anyway.

One of the most popular philosophical movements of the time was Existentialism, which spoke to these pervasive feelings of insecurity with its themes of alienation, despair, absurdity, and meaninglessness. This is the intellectual climate that Kerouac found at university, and he was both seduced and repulsed by it. On the one hand, it resonated with the tragic view of life that he had developed both from Catholicism and from his experiences of poverty, hardship, and death. On the other, his vitalist impulses towards joy and ecstasy and celebration instinctively rebelled against it.

These two opposing moods or currents warred inside of Kerouac all his life. Both found expression in his writing — a surging, vigorous love of life, and a compassionate sadness that stemmed from a recognition of life's impermanence and fragility. In his best moments, he achieves a kind of healthy balance that is akin to the tragic joy of the ancients. But all too often he veers too far in one direction or the other, oscillating between manic hyper-appreciation and hopeless melancholy. There is plenty of decadence, debauchery, and degeneracy to be found in his voluminous writings, and that is what most of his fans today celebrate him for, as a precursor to the cultural revolution of the 1960s. But there is also a reaction and a refusal, a longing for wholesomeness, and for wholeness. Most of Kerouac's critics either miss it or dismiss it, because they don't understand it.

One person who did understand it, eventually, was Kerouac's friend and fellow writer John Clellon Holmes. In his memoir of Kerouac, he wrote, "I never fully understood the hunger that was gnawing in him then, and didn't realize the extent to which the breakup of his Lowell home, the chaos of the war years and the death of his father, had left him disrupted, anchorless; a deeply traditional nature thrown out of kilter, and thus enormously sensitive to anything uprooted, bereft, helpless, or persevering …"[1] How many more young men does that description apply to today? Fatherless, anchorless, thrown out of kilter, enormously sensitive …

My perspective on Kerouac in this essay is largely that which he himself took in his last novel, *Vanity of Duluoz*, written only two years before he drank himself to death at the age of 47. That novel — named after Kerouac's alter ego Jack Duluoz and inspired by the Book of *Ecclesiastes* — is a kind of *mea culpa*; he himself called it his "confession."[2] It concerns the formative years of his life, just after high school when he was awarded a football scholarship to Columbia University and then enrolled in the Navy during the Second World War. The novel makes clear that Kerouac believed his life took a tragic wrong turn at this time, and he explains exactly what that

---

[1] Cited in Paul Maher Jr. *Empty Phantoms: Interviews and Encounters with Jack Kerouac* 124

[2] *Vanity of Duluoz* 261

wrong turn was. This is of significance because his personal wrong turn was also that of the culture as a whole.

1.

TI JEAN

Jack Kerouac was born Jean Louis Lebris de Kerouac in 1922 and grew up in the small working-class town of Lowell, Massachusetts. His ancestors were French-Canadians, and in his later years his genealogy would become very important to him, as the many references to it in his writings and interviews attest. He believed that his ancient ancestors were Celts who had come from Ireland first to Cornwall and then to Brittany. He identified with the Vendean royalist rebels who opposed the French revolution, who fought for "above all the reopening of their parish churches with their former priests."[3] From there his ancestors crossed

[3] Joes, Anthony James *Resisting Rebellion: The History and Politics of Counterinsurgency* University Press of Kentucky, 2006 p. 52-3

the ocean to the new world, settling in Canada. He also believed that he had Iroquois blood.[4]

Many of Kerouac's novels concern his childhood in Lowell. There is *Dr. Sax*, written almost simultaneously with *On The Road*, which is a kind of childhood mythology centered around a mysterious figure called Dr. Sax and a "world serpent" as in Nordic mythology. There is also *Visions of Gerard*, a moving tribute to his older brother who died of rheumatic fever at nine years of age. Finally, *Maggie Cassidy* is the sweet story of a high school romance in a small town.

His mother Gabrielle was a devout Catholic, and she passed her piety on to her son. The Catholic tradition and worldview was one of the largest and most enduring influences on Kerouac, and although he is more often remembered today for his brief but public proclamation of Buddhism

[4] Clark 4-5 and Maher 229-30

in the late 1950s,[5] he never really left the Church. When the *Paris Review* asked him why he wrote about Buddha but not Jesus, he responded incredulously, "I've never written about Jesus? … *all I write about* is Jesus." He was not being flip — the themes and concerns of Catholic theology run very deep all throughout his works. His early concern with matters of faith is well-documented in *Windblown World*, his work journals from the writing of *The Town and the City*, which make clear that he saw his writing as a service to God, and that he approached his craft with the discipline of a monk.

The Lowell of Kerouac's childhood was a mix of French Canadians, Greeks, Eastern Europeans and others. In addition to being a gifted intellect, Kerouac was naturally athletic and graceful, and

[5] Talking about Buddhism in his 1968 interview in *Paris Review*, he sounds almost like Julius Evola: "What's really influenced my work is … the original Buddhism of Gotama Sakyamuni, the Buddha himself, of the India of old … Zen is what's left of his Buddhism, or Bodhi, after its passing into China and then into Japan…. [T]he Buddha (who was of Aryan origin, by the way, I mean Persian warrior caste, and not Oriental as pictured) … He was born in Gorakpur, the son of the consul of the invading Persian hordes. And he was called Sage of the Warriors…" "There is a difference between the original Buddha of India and the Buddha of Vietnam, who just shaves his hair and puts on a yellow robe and is a communist agitating agent."

excelled at sports in his childhood. He was in many ways the embodiment of the ancient maxim *mens sana in corpore sano*. In *Vanity of Duluoz*, he describes his high school self as "a football and track star, a highgrade scholar, independent … good-looking and strong."[6] (One should keep in mind the title of the book, and the fact that Kerouac was no longer any of these things when he wrote this.)

He was given a football scholarship to Columbia University, as a condition of which he had to attend Horace Mann prep school for a year. This is the period of his life covered in *Vanity of Duluoz*. Being accepted to Columbia meant moving to New York. Like many young men, he found himself enthralled by the frenzy of city life — the crowded streets of midtown, the neon lights of Times Square, the jazz clubs of Harlem. In his hunger for experience, he took it all in.

At this stage in his early development, Kerouac very much conceived the world in spiritual terms of light and darkness. His early journals show a remarkably intelligent and sensitive mind, which correctly identified many of the errors in the dominant intellectual currents of the time, such as

[6] *Vanity of Duluoz* 28

their pessimism and immoralism. But, while Kerouac would always fight against the sort of bleakness and negativity that characterized much of atheistic existentialism, his Dionysian streak gave him a weakness for excess and debauchery. Like many others, he experimented with Blake's maxim that "the road of excess leads to the palace of wisdom."

* * * * *

Columbia University at that time was the headquarters of the Frankfurt School of critical theory, which had moved to New York in 1935, after being kicked out of Europe by the National Socialists. The young, healthy, and patriotic Jack Kerouac thus found himself right at ground zero of Antonio Gramsci's "long march through the institutions." He writes indignantly in *Vanity of Duluoz*, "what did Columbia College offer me to study in the way of a course of theirs called Contemporary Civilization but the works of Marx, Engels, Lenin, Russell and other assorted blue-printings that look good on blue paper and all the time the architect is that invisible monster known as Living Man?"[7]

---

[7] *Vanity of Duluoz* 85

What is remarkable about the young Kerouac is how astute he was in his observations of Columbia, the intellectual scene, and his fellow artists who would go on to form the core of the Beat generation. He and his friend Hal Chase developed an understanding of the essential difference between themselves and most of the others in their circle, including Allen Ginsberg and William Burroughs, whom Kerouac met at this time.

Kerouac and Chase were "Wolfeans" — devotees of novelist Thomas Wolfe, who celebrated the greatness of America and of life. Ginsberg and Burroughs, on the other hand, were what Kerouac called "Black Priests," which he described as "sinister European fairy Jew Communists."[8] In addition to these ethnic and sexual differences — Burroughs and Ginsberg were both homosexual — the basic distinction was between those who viewed Western civilization, and specifically its American manifestation, in a positive light, and those who wanted to tear it down. It is this distinction that he returns to in *Vanity of Duluoz*, and which he first developed in another way in his very first novel.

---

[8] Gerald Nicosia, *Memory Babe: A Critical Biography of Jack Kerouac* 156

2.

The First Shall Be Last, and the Last Shall Be First

Kerouac is mostly remembered today for the attitudes that he expressed in his "Road Novels," as the Library of America edition of his works is called. In his quest for experience, freedom, and transcendence, in his advocacy of joy and love, he is regarded as a precursor to the hippy movement. And probably rightly so. Kerouac himself seemed to recognize that he had this influence, and he regretted it and felt guilty for it.

But Kerouac the proto-hippy is not the whole story. What is curious about his trajectory as a writer and thinker is that after his long journey on the road, he ends up in exactly the same place that he began. The values put forward in his last novel, *Vanity of Duluoz*, are almost identical to those in his very first novel, *The Town and the City*.

The Town and the City is modeled on the style of Thomas Wolfe, one of Kerouac's primary inspirations in his early career, and is more conventionally written and also more fictionalized than any of his other works. Those who are only familiar with his later, "spontaneous" and confessional prose style will be surprised by it. The semi-autobiographical sections concern the same period of his life as *Vanity of Duluoz*, but are used in the context of a larger, multi-generational story, which is written in the third person.

The theme of *The Town and the City* is the opposition between simple, morally upright, small town people who have an organic relationship with the land that they work and with each other, and complicated, morally decadent, big city intellectuals who are rootless and alienated. It's a theme entirely congruent with many European reactionary writers, but also with the naturalism of Thoreau and the classical republicanism of Thomas Jefferson, who envisioned an America of independent yeoman farmers.

Oswald Spengler wrote, "If the Early period is characterized by the birth of the City out of the country, and the Late by the battle between city and country, the period of Civilization is that of the victory of city over country, whereby it frees itself from the grip of the ground, but to its own ultimate ruin. Rootless, dead to the cosmic, irrevocably committed to stone and to intellectualism …"[9]

This is precisely the dichotomy which *The Town and the City* explores. For Kerouac, these were two diametrically opposed sets of values, which warred not only in the world at large, but within his own soul.

The Town and the City is set in the fictional town of Galloway, which is a stand-in for Kerouac's hometown of Lowell. It tells the story of the Martin family and their friends and acquaintances, who of course are stand-ins for the Kerouacs and everyone that Jack knew in his life. The Martin family has more children than the Kerouacs, which is both a romanticization of big families and also a literary technique that allowed Kerouac to explore different aspects of his personality through different characters in the Martin family.

The portrayal of Galloway and the Martins is so idyllic that it's reminiscent of Bedford Falls and the Baileys in *It's A Wonderful Life*, at least to 21st century sensibilities. It is idealized, to be sure, but also believable, which makes sense since it is largely based on Kerouac's actual memories. The

[9] *The Decline of the West*: Cities and Peoples 1:VI

people of Galloway are simple and wholesome, industrious and neighborly. Though their lives have much hardship, especially the Martins, the bonds of family and community ultimately make their lives joyous, even in spite of tragedy.

Peter Martin, who represents Kerouac more than any of the other characters, eventually moves to New York City. There, he encounters all the decadence and degeneracy that one would expect. For Kerouac, the primary poisons seemed to be drugs and bad ideas. The "Black Priests" fed him both. This is the second half of the novel, and the first time he set out to describe the mad, crazy, fast-paced complexity of urban life, for which descriptions he would eventually become famous.

Most reviewers of the book nowadays — to the degree that there are any, since most just ignore it altogether — see this as the strong point of the novel, since it anticipates some of his later writing in its descriptions of Times Square and other places. But they seem to miss the larger point of the whole story, that "family is stronger than the evils of modern civilization" as the Sunday Mercury review put it at the time.[10] Perhaps that is one reason why Kerouac sought to reiterate it, in

[10] Brinkley, Introduction to *The Town and the City* xi

his later, more chaotic prose style, in *Vanity of Duluoz*.

The Town and the City is archetypal, but perhaps also merely typical. Throughout history and continuing in the present day, boys and girls from small towns become restless because of what they perceive as the boredom of life in their hometown, and so pack their bags and move to the big city, only to realize later that their hometowns had many virtues which they took for granted. So they move back to a small town or the suburbs to raise their own children, who grow up to become bored and restless there, and the cycle continues.

> "After the first months of his freshman year with its dark campus at night when soft golden light shone in library and lecture room windows, after his wanderings in New York and Philadelphia, he was now returning to something wild and crude, to deep snow and raw gray skies, a flight of dark birds over the pines, to ice-locked brooks and kids skating and shouting in the frosty air, to old woodstoves in saloons and men in boots and jackets, to the New England of towns and woods and snowstorms and deep star-sparkling nights. He realized now with strong conviction that nothing which could be taught him in the university could ever touch the wild joy in his heart, the plain powerful knowledge of things, the boyish glee and wonder he felt now as the train bore him back to the weather and veritable landscape of his soul. He wished

> that he would never leave Galloway again. Nothing that the university taught him could match for him the power and wisdom of his own kind of people, who lived and drew their breath in this rugged land joyous with tidings of towns, plain, homely, genuine and familiar, that he saw rolling by him again."[11]

Perhaps Kerouac thought, as many young men do, that he could dabble in the degeneracy of the modern world for a while before finding his way back to the stability and health of the world of family and tradition. Or perhaps, after seeing his own family struggle and suffer and to some degree fall apart, he felt that this world was off-limits to him, that he had been cast out.

The Town and the City tells the tale of a prodigal son who goes out and gets lost in the big city, but eventually comes home again to Galloway, to Lowell, and to his family. But Kerouac's last novel portrays this story as what it always was: vanity. For as his inspiration Thomas Wolfe said, you can't go home again. Kerouac never lost his longing for a loving family, for a wife and children, and for the simpler, wholesome life of small town America. But he was always thwarted by his longing for adventure, passion, excitement and lust.

---

[11] *The Town and the City* 147

3.

The Influence of Oswald Spengler

Kerouac and Chase had an alternate name for the Black Priests, which was "Baudelaireans," because, like Baudelaire's poetry, they deliberately sought and celebrated evil rather than good. At this time, Burroughs was hanging out in seedy bars in Times Square, befriending pimps and drug dealers, thieves and murderers, who would sometimes store their stolen goods in his apartment. He introduced some of these characters to Kerouac, who was repulsed by them.[12] Nonetheless, in *Vanity of Dulouz* Kerouac is considerably kinder to Burroughs, who is called Will Hubbard in that novel and whom Kerouac calls his "great teacher" and a "Faustian soul."[13] The latter term comes from Oswald Spengler.

---

12 Nicosia 136

13 *Vanity of Duluoz* 204, 199

It's oft-forgotten today that one of the seminal influences on the whole Beat movement was Spengler's *Decline of the West*. One more often thinks of the Beats in the context of French existentialism and the tradition of visionary poets like Blake and Rimbaud. But in fact, both Kerouac and Burroughs were greatly inspired by Spengler's magnum opus, as were so many others during the first half of the 20th century.[14] One could even see the entire Beat movement as either a reaction to Spengler's prophecy of decline, or as a symptom of it, a late-stage religious revival movement of the sort that he describes and predicts.

In *On The Road*, Kerouac describes Old Bull Lee, his fictionalization of Burroughs, as sitting around his house all day reading Spengler. He further says that Burroughs, being older and better educated, acted as a teacher for himself and the others. In *Vanity of Duluoz*, he recalls the day that Burroughs introduced him to Spengler: "Harbinger of the day when we'd become fast friends and he'd

[14] Another counter-cultural writer who was definitively influenced by *Decline of the West* was Henry Miller. The last pages of *Plexus*, the second volume of his *Rosy Crucifixion* trilogy, is a long ode to Spengler and his importance. In his later years, Julius Evola wrote about both Miller and Kerouac, considering both men, ultimately, as decadent, but also seeing some legitimacy in their rebellion against the modern world.

hand me the full two-volume edition of Spengler's *Decline of the West* and say 'EEE di fy your mind, my boy, with the grand actuality of Fact.' "[15]

The "edification" which Burroughs sought to impart via Spengler, and which Kerouac would later come to resent him for, was that the very civilization which Jack loved so deeply and instinctually, was doomed. Hilaire Belloc famously said, "The faith is Europe and Europe is the faith," meaning Catholicism. The decline of the West is therefore also necessarily the decline of the faith. (According to Pat Buchanan's formulation, the decline of the faith comes first, leading to the decline of the culture, and then the civilization, and ultimately the people itself.) For a man like Kerouac, that realization was fatal.

So, under the influence of his mentor Burroughs, Kerouac accepted Spengler's thesis that his civilization, the Western European-American civilization, was in terminal decline. For Spengler, culture is an organism, and its life cycle of birth, growth, decay and death is as certain and inevitable as that of a human being. The notion of decay and death would have had a strong resonance with Kerouac at this point in his life, since his father

[15] *Vanity of Duluoz* 204

was going through a long and painful battle with stomach cancer and would pass away two years later in 1946. Indeed, he begins *On The Road* by relating that it was his sadness after his father's death that gave rise to the restless feelings that pushed him onto the road in the first place.

That Kerouac never really got over the death of his father in his youth is made clear in *Vanity of Duluoz*, where he relates that the death of his father taught him the true meaning of Jesus' words on the cross, "Father, why has thou forsaken me?"[16] Furthermore, he relates this to the "death of God" which was (and still is) the dominant theme of Western culture. The death of religion and religious values, the death of fatherhood and patriarchy, the death of God the Father, and the death of Leo Kerouac the Father — for Jack all of these are the fist blows of life in "late civilization," analogically

[16] *Vanity of Duluoz* 263

and archetypically interconnected.[17] And it should also be remembered that the last years of Kerouac's life were also the years of Vatican II and so, some traditionalists would say, the last years of the true Catholic Church.

With the death of Catholicism and the West, Kerouac now had only scraps to pick from. He chose Spengler's notion of the *fellaheen*. *Fellah* is an Arabic word meaning "peasant farmer"; *fellaheen* is the plural. Spengler used the term to describe the people who persist after a civilization has collapsed. He often writes of them as analogous to primitive peoples, insofar as both are

---

[17] Kerouac was, as some of his friends have noted, a mythologizer, someone who tried to see the traces of eternity in time and divinity in the mundane. In this way, there is a curious parallel between him and the Chilean writer Miguel Serrano, who also mythologized the events of his life to give them greater significance. (Serrano talks about the importance of actively bestowing meaning in his book on *Nietzsche and the Eternal Return*.) One difference between the two men's approaches is that for Serrano, the events of ordinary life only matter insofar as they conform to timeless archetypes. Thus, his childhood best friend becomes Jason of Greek mythology, his youthful love is a Valkyrie, and the Second World War is a parallel to the Mahabharata. For Kerouac, the people and events of his life are equally important, but just as they are, without need of reference to archetypes or other stories. One imagines that if he had had Serrano's mythopoetic sensibility, he would have written of Neal Cassady as an avatar of Dionysus or Loki.

underdeveloped and lowly. But whereas a primitive people exists at the beginning of a historical cycle, a fellaheen people exists at its end. "And that which follows a Culture we may call — from its best known example, the Egyptians of post-Roman times — fellah peoples."[18]

> At this level all Civilizations enter upon a stage, which lasts for centuries, of appalling depopulation. The whole pyramid of cultural man vanishes. It crumbles from the summit, first the world cities, then the provincial forms, and finally the land itself, whose best blood has incontinently poured into the towns, merely to bolster them up awhile. At the last, only the primitive blood remains, alive, but robbed of its strongest and most promising elements. This residue is the Fellah type.[19]

The fellah is the human being reduced to a base existence. "Life as experienced by primitive and by fellaheen peoples is just the zoological up and down, a planless happening without goal or cadenced march in time, wherein occurrences are many, but, in the last analysis, devoid of significance."[20]

---

[18] *The Decline of the West* (DW): Cities and Peoples 1:V

[19] DW: Cities and Peoples 1:V

[20] DW: Cities and Peoples 3:III

In Kerouac's writing, fellaheen becomes an adjective almost synonymous with beat. One can see the sort of stoned syllogism he formulated: the fellaheen are the beaten and downtrodden; "beat" also means "beatific;" therefore, the fellaheen, the lumpen, the outcasts, are holy. Most of his writing from the mid 1950s through the early 60s is filled with this romantic notion of the underclass, no doubt derived in part from Christian teachings about the blessedness of the poor, and the vows of poverty taken by monastics. Taking his stoner logic a step further, Kerouac seemed to reason that if monks volunteer for poverty in order to attain sainthood, then perhaps those who are poor are already saints, or at least closer to it than the rich and middle-class. It is, after all, easier for a camel to pass through the eye of a needle than for a rich man to enter the Kingdom of God.

In *Desolation Angels*, he wrote: "One look at the officials in the American Consulate where we went for dreary paper routines was enough to make you realize what was wrong with American 'diplomacy' throughout the Fellaheen world: - stiff officious squares with contempt even for their own Americans who happened not to wear neckties, as tho a necktie or whatever it stands for meant anything to the hungry Berbers who came into

Tangiers every Saturday morning on meek asses, like Christ, carrying baskets of pitiful fruit or dates, and returned at dusk to silhouetted parades along the hill by the railroad track."

Much of Kerouac's early adult life was spent traveling and exploring various fellaheen locations, looking for holiness there. He went to New York and hung out with the hustlers and drug addicts of Times Square and Harlem, apparently having gotten over his initial revulsion. He drank with winos and bums in Denver and San Francisco. He went to Mexico, which he regarded as quintessentially fellaheen, in its poverty, its rural peasantry, and its racial *mestizaje*. Spengler wrote that the fellaheen is "raceless." For Kerouac, it seemed to mean simply poor and non-white, leading to his famous "wishing I were a Negro" passage quoted earlier.

To the end of his life, Kerouac interpreted the Beat movement in Spenglerian terms; indeed, he interpreted the whole 20th century that way.

4.

Kerouac and Ginsberg

In *Vanity of Duluoz* Kerouac writes about the first time he and Allen Ginsberg met. "One look at him, a few days of knowing him to avouch my private claim, and I came to the conclusion he was a lecher who wanted everybody in the world to take a bath in the same huge bathtub which would give him a chance to feel legs under the dirty water. This is precisely the image I had of him on first meeting."[21] Nonetheless, in spite of Kerouac's initial impression of him, he and Ginsberg became close friends, largely because both were writers and poets obsessed with their craft.

Neither Ginsberg nor Burroughs achieved the level of fame that Kerouac did in the late 1950s and early 1960s. This is partly because, of the three, Kerouac was the least counter-cultural, the least anti-American in sentiment and purpose. To

[21] *Vanity of Duluoz* 212

the contrary, he had a deep love of America as land, as place — *On The Road* is basically a prose love poem to America — which naturally translated itself into conservative political leanings, albeit of a nonconventional sort. (He famously watched the McCarthy hearings while getting high on marijuana and cheering for McCarthy.)

Burroughs and Ginsberg, on the other hand, found their true audience in the counter-culture of the mid to late 1960s. In contrast to Kerouac, neither had an instinct for patriotism — quite the opposite, in fact. Burroughs was a cynical nihilist for whom patriotism was simply one more "junk con," — he famously described military men as simopaths: "a man convinced he is an ape or other simian" — while Ginsberg was a New York Jewish communist who grew up on radicalism and critical theory, a true child of the Frankfurt School. His famous poem "America," published in *Howl*, is full of the sort of invective one still hears from leftists and SJWs to this day. In the 60s, Ginsberg became a leader of the hippie movement and promoted Eastern religions, psychedelic drugs, protest, "free love," and gay liberation. Later, he became a member of the pro-pedophilia group NAMBLA, as well as a university professor in New York City (the former apparently poses no career limitations for the latter) where he was known for his sexual pursuits of his male students, confirming Kerouac's initial impressions of him.

Burroughs likewise embraced 60s radicalism, though not with the same values as Ginsberg. A lifelong anti-liberal and gun enthusiast, he preferred violent revolutionary groups to hippy peace activists. Nonetheless, the counter-culture embraced him for his critique of bureaucracy, of white racism, and his open homosexuality, which often bordered on pedophilia — Burroughs was a "sexpat" who spent years living in the Third World in order to have easier access to drugs and teenage male prostitutes. Burroughs' nihilism, in contrast to Ginsberg's leftist idealism, later gave him an audience with the punk rock scene, on which he had a rather large influence.

The essential difference between Kerouac and the others was summed up by Jack in an exchange with hippie activist Ed Sanders on William Buckley's *Firing Line* program in 1968: "I made myself famous by writing songs and lyrics about the beauty of the things I did, and the ugliness too. You made yourself famous by saying, 'Down with this, down with that, throw eggs at this, throw eggs at that!' " He may as well have been talking to Ginsberg, which in a way he was since Ginsberg was present in the audience and was an ally of Sanders.

After Sanders mentions Ginsberg chanting *aum* in the streets, Kerouac turns to him and says, "Beware of false prophets who come unto you dressed in sheep's clothing, and underneath they are ravening wolves."

"But who's that?" Sanders asks. The bell rings to signal a commercial break before we can hear if Kerouac answered, but it's obvious he was referring to Ginsberg.

* * * * *

On The Road was published in 1957 and was an instant success, due largely to a very positive review in the *New York Times* by Gilbert Millstein. For a while, Jack enjoyed the attention and the new opportunities that came his way, such as making recordings of his poetry and prose with jazz musicians accompanying him. But he was not prepared for the barrage of negative reaction that came soon afterward, with critics dismissing his book as having no substance and his writing style as having no discipline. Truman Capote famously quipped, "That's not writing, that's typewriting."

Aside from the reaction by the literary establishment, there was also the hijacking of the

Beat movement by elements that Kerouac neither agreed with nor approved of. In his Paris Review interview with Ted Berrigan, he said

> Oh the Beat generation was just a phrase I used in the 1951 written manuscript of *On the Road* to describe guys like Moriarty who run around the country in cars looking for odd jobs, girlfriends, kicks. It was thereafter picked up by West Coast Leftist groups and turned into a meaning like "Beat mutiny" and "Beat insurrection" and all that nonsense; they just wanted some youth movement to grab on to for their own political and social purposes. I had nothing to do with any of that. I was a football player, a scholarship college student, a merchant seaman, a railroad brakeman on road freights, a script synopsizer, a secretary ... And Moriarty-Cassady was an actual cowboy on Dave Uhl's ranch in New Raymer, Colorado ... What kind of beatnik is that?"[22]

"Beat," as Kerouac originally conceived of it, was a fundamentally religious disposition. The word is a double entendre referring to both being beaten down and also beatitude. To be beat was to be a seeker, and *On The Road* is the story of a religious quest, however confused or misguided it may be. But the media conception of the "beatnik" that came to predominate had nothing to do with this, and was instead a shallow caricature of youths

---

[22] *Conversations with Jack Kerouac* p78-79.

who like jazz music, French cigarettes, and easy women. The television character Dobie Gillis is the obvious example.

It was this caricature of the Beats that became the inspiration for the 60s counterculture more than Kerouac's actual vision. In 1968 Kerouac explained the counterculture to William F. Buckley as "apparently some kind of Dionysian movement in late civilization, and which I did not intend, any more than I suppose Dionysus did … although I'm not Dionysius the Areopagite. I should have been." The point — that Kerouac's sensibilities and values are religious like Dionysius the Areopagite, not chaotic and destructive like the god Dionysus — flies right over Buckley's head. Kerouac, even in his inebriated state, is still the more erudite of the two.

In 1964, he wrote to an Italian journalist,

> What these bozos and their friends are up to now is simply the last act in their original adoption and betrayal of any truly "beat" credo. They have used "beat" for their own ends, like Lawrence Lipton and even Miller have done. Why, I don't know, except to point out they can't possibly feel the way I do about life because their childhoods were distorted by madness and disorder, and mine was not. Now that we're all getting to be middleaged I can see that they're just frustrated hysterical provocateurs and attention-seekers with nothing on their

> mind but rancor towards "America" and the life of ordinary people. They have never written about ordinary people with any love, you may have noticed. ... Genet and Burroughs do not offend half as much, because they are metaphysically hopeless; but Ginsberg and Corso are ignorant enough to be metaphysically healthy and want to use art as a racket. Ginsberg was just on TV announcing the imminent "Fall of America," for instance; and Corso visited me last summer wanting "my riches," wanting to move his wife into my mother s house, wanting one of my adolescent novels to use as his own, finally announcing that I was as good as dead because I do not want to parade with him and Ginsberg politically. And I've felt this coming on ever since 1956. I don't know where they got all this, or what they do behind my back, or even say about me behind my back, but I've always felt something funny about the two of them "behind me" and Orlovsky too.

Despite their substantial disagreements, Ginsberg and Kerouac remained friends, perhaps a reflection of loyalty on both their parts. But Jack was right to feel "something funny" about Ginsberg's support of him. Ever since Kerouac's death in 1969, Ginsberg has been one of the primary shapers of the Kerouac legacy, ensuring that he is remembered not as a right-wing Catholic but as New Age Buddhist exponent of free love and hedonism.

Compared to Ginsberg, Kerouac was deeply conservative. But *On The Road* did in fact pave the way for the hippies, and I think Kerouac realized this and felt both ashamed and guilty for it. The dominant view of Kerouac today is that he sort of went half-way into radicalism, and is therefore half-praiseworthy. We can like him for extolling sex and drugs and jazz, but his Catholicism and conservatism and anti-Semitism are most unfortunate. Perhaps he was not sexually liberated enough — Ginsberg says in his introduction to *Visions of Cody* that Kerouac and Neal Cassady should have become lovers, that it would have "done them some good." Indeed, there is an entire revisionist biography of Kerouac by Ellis Amburn claiming that Kerouac was a repressed homosexual and that this is the key to his work. But while there is ample documentation of Kerouac's homosexual dalliances over the years, it's glaringly obvious that he preferred women. Furthermore, Amburn like many contemporary commentators shows a real lack of understanding of masculinity, reading "gay subtexts" into male friendships in order to deconstruct and subvert them.[23]

What Ginsberg and to a lesser extent Burroughs could never understand about Kerouac was his love of tradition: Catholicism, family, patriotism, and in his later years, his European Celtic heritage. There was the other side of him as well, the drunken dissolute who seemed to thrive on chaos — but these two sides were always at war in Kerouac, which is why he died so much younger than the other Beat writers, for whom there was no such conflict because they were firmly on the side of modernity and subversion.

Kerouac wrote to Ginsberg of the essential differences between them in 1957:

> Allen, you know why I said I was greatest American poet and you greatest Israeli poet? Because you didn't pick up on Americana till you read VISIONS OF NEAL, before that you were big Burroughsian putter-downer of Americana. Remember Hal Chase and the Wolfeans and the Dark Priests? You suddenly saw Americana of Neal and all, and picked up on it, and made a killing on it, but your heart's in the mountains, O Tribe of the Mountains, the Mountains of Judea! Am I not right? YOU KNOW

---

[23] Revisionist biographies which reimagine historical figures as homosexual are virtually a cottage industry at this point, with both Friedrich Nietzsche and Adolf Hitler having been subjects of similar attempts.

I'M RIGHT. Burroughs' own Americana is effortless, it's Brad coming on their redleather seat, so he is intrinsically Americana, like me (with teenage poems to Americana) but you only got in the act later. This is pure vision of Ginsberg's poetry history. Because you are not an American, you are a Magian man, and belong to the yearning new culture of the 21st century, which will be Magian, Orthodoxy, Cavern-feeling ... s'why old tired Western Franciscan monks of Italy can't convince you, because you are really an Arab and above all an Aramean Russian Motherlander. Jews and Arabs are Semites, and Jews and Arabs and Russians are all Orthodox in the deepest sense.[24]

[24] Letter to Allen Ginsberg, December 10, 1957, in *Selected Letters 1957-1969*.

5.

Kerouac and the Jews

"The Germans should not have been our 'enemies'. I say this and stake my life on it." [25]

"... the Communist is the main enemy - the Jew." [26]

Jack Kerouac, at the end of his life

At the time of Kerouac's attendance at Horace Mann prep school, ninety-six percent of the students there were Jewish, "most from wealthy families."[27] Before this Kerouac didn't have much experience with Jews, except that his father had warned him to be wary of them. Indeed, one of Leo Kerouac's last admonitions to his son was "Beware of the niggers and the Jews."[28]

---

[25] *Vanity of Duluoz* 132

[26] Tom Clark, *Jack Kerouac: A Biography* 216

[27] Nicosia 62

[28] Nicosia 163

Today Kerouac's biographers tend to dismiss his undeniable anti-semitism as both an unfortunate inheritance from his father and also a by-product of his late-life disillusionment, ill temper, and alcoholic paranoia. But it's clear from the above 1957 letter, and from Kerouac's life and work as a whole, that he was not some simple-minded bigot who merely "hated Jews." Rather, he had an understanding of Jews as having an outsider and oppositional status in traditional American culture, a status rooted in their opposition to Christianity — something he would have learned about from the pre-Vatican II Catholic Church — and also their ethnic differences with Western Europeans. He saw the distinction in Spenglerian terms, which classifies Western European civilization as "Faustian," and Near-Eastern civilization as "Magian."

It's remarkable that he saw that 21st century culture and spirituality would not be "American," which in this context means Western European and Faustian, but would be "Magian," of the East, and of a type which rather than promoting the heroism and individualism of Faustian man, promotes the dissolution of the individual ego into the greater collective Spirit. Kerouac is usually understood as a herald of this coming new age, but the truth of the matter is that, while he did see its coming very clearly, he lamented it, however much he may have tried to celebrate it sometimes. His heart was always with the "Western Franciscan monks," with Americana.

In his last article, prophetically titled "After Me, The Deluge" and published less than a month before he died, Kerouac wonders "how I could possibly spawn Jerry Rubin, Mitchell Goodman, Abbie Hoffman, Allen Ginsberg, and other warm human beings from the ghettos who say they suffered no less than the Puerto Ricans in their barrios and the blacks in their Big and Little Harlems, and all because I wrote a matter-of-fact account of a true adventure on the road (hardly an agitational propaganda account) featuring an ex-cowhand and an ex-footballer driving across the continent ..."[29]

What most commenters on Kerouac miss is that every single hippie activist he names is Jewish, and he is calling them out for attaching themselves to black and Puerto Rican movements and agitating for civil unrest. He felt that certain radical Jews, including Allen Ginsberg, had done the same to

---

[29] http://archives.chicagotribune.com/1969/09/28/page/222/article/after-me-the-deluge

him and to the Beat movement. His friend and fellow poet Gregory Corso later said, "He had this funny idea that Jews were crowding in and taking his Beat generation over. This was towards the end."[30]

Kurt Vonnegut also recalled meeting Kerouac sometime in the late 60s, and that Kerouac said "that Jews were the real Nazis, and that Allen Ginsberg had been told by the Communists to befriend Kerouac in order that they might gain control of American young people ..."[31]

Ginsberg, to his credit, acknowledged that Kerouac was not without justification in his feelings. In his interview for the 1986 documentary *What Happened to Kerouac?*, Ginsberg stated:

> Jack was [anti-Semitic], but sort of rightfully because he was being attacked constantly by all the New York Jewish intellectuals, who did have a vendetta against him. Beginning with a guy named Bernstein, an editor of the *New York Times* who *hated* Kerouac, according to family gossip brought to us by Ernest von Hartz, a co-editor on the *New York Times*, who said that Bernstein was so afraid and scared of Kerouac that he did everything he could to smudge his name in the New York Times. ... Or to leave

---

[30] *What Happened to Kerouac?* Disc 2 extras, interview with Allen Ginsberg

[31] *Palm Sunday* p. 230

him prey to attack by anyone who wanted to attack him."[32]

A passage in volume 2 of Kerouac's *Selected Letters* refers to these critics and their attacks:

> Jack was so "sick and tired of being insulted by critics," he told Carolyn Cassady on October 21, 1962, that he "just about decided not to publish any more.... They make me sick with their Jew talk.... They'll go around vaunting their Philip Roths and Herbert Golds and Bernard Malamuds and J.D. Salingers and Saul Bellowses, whilst the bestselling is being taken care of by Micheners and Wouks, and my only clientele are kids who steal my books in bookstores." [33]

In other words, the largely Jewish literary establishment in New York was a self-congratulatory club whose members spent all their time praising each other's works while denigrating Kerouac, an outsider to their club, as a writer of hoodlum literature.

Jack complained in a letter to John Clellon Holmes:

> I just brooding stagnant angry relic of the past. I not big Jewish genius like Saul Bellow, Philip Roth, Irwin Shaw,

---

[32] *What Happened to Kerouac?* Disc 2 extras, interview with Allen Ginsberg

[33] *Selected Letters 1957-1969* p. 345

> Herman Wouk, Norman Mailer, Bernard Malamud, J. D. Salinger—I big tin-eared Canuck with royalty check of $1.37 last week, and $15.19 week before—I no have standing in American literature with above mentioned American Giants because I not really a 'writer,' just a phenomena and according to fan letters asking if I am real, unreal anyhow. I not 'American' like above but some kind 'nik.'
>
> Worked out fine by Podhoretz and swell critics and Van Doren great helpin' mentor also Cowley.
>
> Krim say I immigrant like him, because my Pop come from 3 miles north of Maine. [34]

Kerouac was essentially used and then abused by this literary establishment, and then spit out by them and promptly forgotten. After the overnight success of *On The Road* in 1957, his subsequent novels were met with derision and dismissal by the literary establishment, even though he served as the inspiration for many of the subsequent trends in American popular culture. In 1961 he wrote Sterling Lord:

> I feel that Route 66 and Al Zugsmith and all that represents the fact that my ideas are being lifted left and right, depriving me of maybe a million, and just between you and me being lifted by Jews, I should really subtitle

[34] Kerouac to John Clellon Holmes, March 2, 1965

> Big Sur: Another Idea for the Jews to Steal—But of course I wont— dont wanta be blackballed … [35]

Kerouac's resentment against Jewish critics and Jewish radicals was on display during his appearance on William F. Buckley's *Firing Line* in 1968. He appeared alongside Lewis Yablonsky, a Jewish professor of sociology who apparently symbolized in Kerouac's mind the type of critic and academic that had been a source of trouble for him. Kerouac, already quite drunk by the beginning of the show, viciously trolls Yablonsky the entire time. He rolls his eyes and gives a thumbs down to the audience during Yablonsky's comments. He interrupts him to correct his pronunciation, mocking his professorial pretension. He makes goofy noises and has to be shushed by Buckley — it's all quite hilarious to see. Finally, near the end of the show, he refers to him as "Abramowitz or whatever his name is," to which Yablonsky responds, "Don't be anti-semitic with me. I happen to be Jewish. My name is Yablonsky."

Kerouac turns to look him directly in the eyes and says, "That's the classic answer isn't it." Buckley asks him to elaborate but he changes the subject. However, it's clear that he was referring to

---

[35] Kerouac letter to Sterling Lord, October 9, 1961

the charge of anti-semitism — the classic answer, or accusation, of Jews who don't want to be criticized.

* * * * *

When one considers Kerouac's many statements on Jewish critics and Jewish radicals, together with his Spenglerian view of European history and ancestry, the fact is that Kerouac is much more a precursor of the 21st century dissident Right than he is of any left-wing counterculture or new age pseudo-spirituality.

6.

The End

What really matters in Kerouac is not who or what he was against, but what he was for. And what was that? In the same interview with Buckley, he spelled out his beliefs and his vision for the Beat Generation clearly and succinctly: "I believe in order, tenderness, and piety."

Order as against chaos, such as the chaos he saw being promoted by the 60s revolutionaries, and perhaps more sinister elements using them from the shadows. Tenderness, meaning love and compassion, sympathy for one's fellow man, decency, and charity in the original sense of *caritas*. Piety, meaning faithfulness and loyalty, and above all love and devotion to God. All of this leads back to order, to order in the soul of man, which is something Kerouac never quite found in this life, but he had sense enough to know to seek it, and not to be satisfied with any of the falsities and temptations of this world.

The Beat movement, he said to Buckley, was intended to be centered on "beatitude, pleasure in life, and tenderness." What Kerouac was searching for, and what he thought he found in a figure like Neal Cassady, was a fusion of the intellect with physicality, like Byron's ideal of the cultured thug. His vision, which above all was vitalistic, was a rebellion against both the gnostic, anti-physical tendencies of religion and the dour, melancholic tendencies of bookish intellectualism. The great irony and tragedy is that Kerouac himself very much embodied this ideal as a young man. It was only when he went astray, into the intellectual and literary currents of his day, and into the drugs and alcohol which always represent a temptation for writers and artists, that he lost this ideal.

Although it's common to say that Kerouac drank himself to death, as I myself wrote at the beginning of this essay, the truth of the matter — hardly ever mentioned — is that he died as a result of injuries sustained in a bar fight. In his 1970 eulogy for Kerouac in *Esquire* magazine, Jack McClintock wrote, "A few weeks before he died in St. Petersburg, Florida, he and a friend went out (as he rarely did), drank too much, and were beaten up by several angry blacks in a ghetto bar. I think it never occurred to Kerouac that he was not wanted there, not in these times."[36] Kerouac's internal organs were already damaged by alcohol, but it seems highly likely that this beating hastened his demise.

There is of course a great irony to the fact that Jack Kerouac, the man who wrote of "wishing he was a negro," died as the victim of black-on-white violence. That irony would not have been lost on Kerouac himself, who in his last years had thoroughly adopted what Spanish philosopher Miguel de Unamuno called the "tragic view of life."

He spent his last years writing and also painting, often religious imagery. Some of those late writings have recently been published by the Library of America in a volumed entitled *The Unknown Kerouac.* His final testament, though, was *Vanity of Duluoz*, in which he takes himself to task for getting involved with the Black Priests and Baudelaireans, for not returning to Lowell as his early alter ego Peter Martin had. There is one particularly poignant scene in which Jack and his friends are laying around the house, high on drugs,

---

[36] Maher 376

doing nothing, and are seen by a returning WW2 veteran, who looks upon them with disgust and incomprehension. It is really Kerouac looking back on his younger self, the veteran representing the best of what he could have been, and the best of the country he loved.

> I can never forget how June's present husband, Harry Evans, suddenly came clomping down the hall of her apartment in his Army boots, fresh from the German front, around September 1945, and was appalled to see us, six fullgrown people, all high on Benny sprawled and sitting and cat-legged on that vast double-doublebed of "skepticism" and "decadence," discussing the nothingness of values, pale-faced, weak bodies, Gad the poor guy said: "This is what I fought for?" His wife told him to come down from his "character heights" or some such. He divorced her awhile later. Of course we know the same thing was going on in Paris and Berlin of the same month and year, now that we've read Günther Grass and Uwe Johnson and Sartre and even, of course, Auden and his *Age of Anxiety*. [37]

We should read Kerouac for both his virtues and his flaws, especially because he himself was so aware of his flaws and so honest about many of them. His legacy is much obscured by the mythology of the Beat generation and the enduring

---

[37] *Vanity of Duluoz* 271

influence of the Baby Boomer generation and its values of hedonism and licentiousness, but the core of his writing is a testament to great love of man and country, and of life itself, a grand and ecstatic celebration of life in its beauty and its sadness.

BIBLIOGRAPHY

Works by Jack Kerouac

The Town and the City (New York: Penguin Classics 2000)

On The Road (New York: Penguin Classics 1999)

Dr. Sax (New York: Grove Press, 1994)

Visions of Gerard (New York: Penguin Books 1991)

Maggie Cassidy (New York: Penguin Books 1993)

Visions of Cody (New York: Penguin Books 1993)

Desolation Angels (New York: Penguin Books 1995)

Vanity of Duluoz (New York: Penguin Books, 1994)

"After Me, The Deluge" http://archives.chicagotribune.com/1969/09/28/page/222/article/after-me-the-deluge

Windblown World (New York: Penguin 2006)

Selected Letters 1957-1969 (New York: Penguin 2000)

Interview with Ted Berrigan, *The Paris Review* No. 43, Summer 1968

Other Works Cited

Clark, Tom *Jack Kerouac* (New York: Harcourt, Brace, Jovanovich, 1984)

Maher Jr., Paul *Empty Phantoms: Interviews and Encounters with Jack Kerouac* (New York: Thunder's Mouth Press, 2005)

Nicosia, Gerald *Memory Babe: A Critical Biography of Jack Kerouac* (New York: Grove Press, 1983)

Spengler, Oswald *The Decline of the West* trans. Charles Francis Atkinson (London: George Allen & Unwin Ltd., 1932)
Vonnegut, Kurt *Palm Sunday* (New York: The Dial Press, 1981; 2006)

What Happened to Kerouac? Two-disc DVD set. Shout Factory, 2012
Firing Line television program, Episode 113, "The Hippies," Recorded on September 3, 1968. Available online

Printed in Great Britain
by Amazon

44166975R00038